THE MANAGING RECRUITMENT POCKETBOOK

C000102831

By Stewart Wright and John Sponton

Drawings by Phil Hailstone

"An invaluable reference tool that will help you get the best for the best."
Julie MacDonald, HR Director, PizzaExpress

"An invaluable and easily digestible guide, packed with useful tips for recruiting the right people for your business."
Mike Winstone, BA, MCIPD, HR Director (Cable), Telewest Broadband

Published by:
Management Pocketbooks Ltd
Laurel House, Station Approach, Alresford, Hants SO24 9JH, U.K.
Tel: +44 (0)1962 735573   Fax: +44 (0)1962 733637
E-mail: sales@pocketbook.co.uk
Website: www.pocketbook.co.uk

This edition published 2005.

British Library Cataloguing-in-Publication Data – A catalogue record for this book is available from the British Library.

ISBN 1 903776 34 1

Design, typesetting and graphics by **efex ltd**. Printed in UK

CONTENTS

CONTINUED

CONTENTS

1NTRODUCTION

DOES RECRUITMENT FEEL LIKE A GAMBLE?

Think back to the recruitment you have handled, or when you have been applying for jobs.

Did it feel any better for you?

INTRODUCTION

<u>SIMPLE</u> TECHNIQUES WILL GO A LONG WAY

Structure your recruitment – be clear on the skills the successful candidate needs to have, and plan each part of the recruitment process.

Imagine yourself in the candidate's shoes when designing your process.

Map out what you want to achieve from each stage of the recruitment process – leave nothing to chance.

Prepare in advance, particularly for your interviews.

Learn about the legal implications which need to be followed – these will help you to recruit more fairly and effectively.

Enable your candidates to give of their best and to show their potential.

REWARD FOR YOUR EFFORTS

Effective recruitment is a skill, and like all skills, takes time and effort to master.

Apply the ground rules, mix with some common sense, planning and preparation to make a winning recipe: a successful candidate who achieves results for your organisation!

KNOWING WHAT YOU WANT
& GETTING IT RIGHT

KNOWING WHAT YOU WANT & GETTING IT RIGHT

BENEFITS

Recruiting successful candidates helps you achieve certain goals:

For the organisation
- Improved performance
- Increased customer satisfaction
- A better reputation
- Greater staff morale

For you
- A reputation for being able to recruit effectively

KNOWING WHAT YOU WANT & GETTING IT RIGHT

THE JOB PROFILE

The key first stage is to be clear on what the job actually entails.

If you have an old job description, do not assume that this will still be valid.

Start instead with a blank sheet of paper, and write down:

- **The job title**
- **The job purpose** – Why does the job exist? How does it benefit the organisation?
- **The job scope** – Who will the job report to? How many people will the post holder manage? How large is the post holder's budget?
- **The job duties** – What are the key tasks and responsibilities of the job?

THE PERSON PROFILE

Building up a picture of the job to be filled will probably have started you thinking about the skills needed. Your task now is to build upon the information in the job profile and to decide what **personal attributes are essential and desirable for good job performance**.

Attributes can mean experience, qualifications, knowledge, skills or competencies – anything which makes the person successful in the role you have just defined. The following pages will expand on each of the areas, and give you some guidelines to help you think about what areas to cover.

THE PERSON PROFILE

Use a table like this to help you structure the person profile:

	Essential	Desirable
Experience gained		
Knowledge		
Qualifications		
Skills/competencies		

KNOWING WHAT YOU WANT & GETTING IT RIGHT

THE PERSON PROFILE

ITEM 1
ITEM 2
ITEM 3
ITEM 4
ITEM 5

Essential means **'must have'**. Any candidate lacking in this area should be rejected.

Desirable means **'nice to have'**. Candidates possessing these qualities bring an additional benefit, and this could be used to distinguish between candidates who meet **all** of the **essential** requirements.

Ask yourself, whenever you put something in the Essential column:
'Is this quality absolutely essential? If it was lacking, what would be the likely effect on job performance?'

THE PERSON PROFILE

Experience

- What type and length of work experience is required to do this job?
- What success or achievements would there need to be evidence of?
- What type of organisations might the candidate have worked for?
- What level of responsibility should the candidate have held to date?

Knowledge

- What knowledge of particular markets/sectors/types of organisations is needed?
- What type and level of knowledge is required to do this job, eg particular products, processes or systems?
- Does the successful candidate need to be familiar with certain computer systems or packages from their first day of employment?

KNOWING WHAT YOU WANT & GETTING IT RIGHT

THE PERSON PROFILE

Qualifications

- Academic qualifications – what level, which ones, how many?
- Vocational qualifications
- Professional qualifications
- Other qualifications if relevant, eg driving licence?

KNOWING WHAT YOU WANT & GETTING IT RIGHT

THE PERSON PROFILE

Skills/competencies

Skills are those qualities acquired through a combination of learning and training. Eg:

- A particular technical skill such as welding
- A particular managerial skill such as project management

Competencies describe particular behaviours or abilities. They are written in a way to help managers assess candidates during a recruitment process. For example, this is a competency for team working:

- Gives help and active support to colleagues
- Does their fair share of work
- Takes on work willingly
- Tries their hand at different tasks to benefit the team

THE PERSON PROFILE

There are lists of management and professional competencies covering such areas as leadership, persuasive communication, problem solving, drive, resilience, and flexibility, amongst others.

Think about which **skills** and **competencies** are important for this role; have a go at defining them in a sentence or two and write them in your person profile as **essential** or **desirable**.

KNOWING WHAT YOU WANT & GETTING IT RIGHT

RECRUITMENT & THE LAW

ITEM 1
ITEM 2
ITEM 3
ITEM 4
ITEM 5

Your recruitment process must work within the law so as not to unfairly advantage or disadvantage certain candidates, and to protect both yourself and your organisation. And working within the law also helps you to recruit and select effectively.

There are two important concepts underpinning recruitment legislation – **direct discrimination**, and **indirect discrimination**. Both types of discrimination in recruitment are **illegal** in the UK.

Direct discrimination is treating a person, or a group, less favourably than others. For example, not offering a job to a man because of his gender; or refusing to offer a job to a candidate because he/she is from a particular racial group.

Indirect discrimination is applying a condition that certain groups are less likely to be able to meet. For example, stating that 'Candidates need to be over 5'6" tall', when it has no bearing on doing the job effectively! Women as a group are proportionately less likely to be over 5'6" than men. If you cannot justify the height requirement, this is indirect discrimination.

KNOWING WHAT YOU WANT & GETTING IT RIGHT

RECRUITMENT & THE LAW

CURRENT LEGISLATION

The following legislation makes direct and indirect discrimination unlawful in the relevant area:

- Sex Discrimination Act (1976)
- Race Relations Act (1986)
- Disability Discrimination Act (1995)
- Employment Equality Act (Sexual Orientation) (2003)
- Employment Equality Act (Religion and Belief) (2003)

Discrimination on the grounds of age will shortly be added to this list on the basis that the government remains on course for its age legislation to be introduced on 1 October 2006. From a recruitment perspective, this means that the legislation will ban unjustified age discrimination.

RECRUITMENT & THE LAW

CONDITIONS

Applying a condition which results in direct or indirect discrimination is unlawful unless the condition can be **justified**.

For example, a person who works in a warehouse might need to lift heavy weights as an essential part of the job. The job and person profile would reinforce the justification of this requirement.

Certain groups – but only a few – are exempt from the relevant legislation on the grounds of safety or decency, for example, public lavatory attendants. Also, some organisations are allowed to show discrimination when recruiting if it is important to the nature of their business. For example, a Chinese restaurant may feel it needs to recruit Chinese waiters.

If a recruitment decision was challenged, the onus would rest on the employer to justify why that person was not appointed.

ITEM 1
ITEM 2
ITEM 3
ITEM 4
ITEM 5

KNOWING WHAT YOU WANT & GETTING IT RIGHT

RECRUITMENT & THE LAW
DISABILITY

Specific to the Disability Discrimination Act, you need to make any **reasonable adjustments** in your recruitment processes to ensure that a disabled person is not at a disadvantage.

For example, when inviting a candidate with special requirements to an interview or assessment process, ask the individual in advance what steps can be taken to help them give of their best on the recruitment day.

KNOWING WHAT YOU WANT & GETTING IT RIGHT

RECRUITMENT & THE LAW

DATA PROTECTION

Another key piece of legislation is the **Data Protection Act**. Individuals have a right of access, upon request, to any information relating to them (either stored on paper or electronically). The act covers the collection, holding, use and destruction of the data.

To stay within the spirit of the legislation:

- Limit the questions and the screening criteria you apply to the areas covered on your job and person profiles and ensure that these are relevant and justifiable
- Keep full and relevant records (including interview notes) of your recruitment process, but do not keep these for longer than is justifiable or reasonable

Most employers would hold recruitment information for 12 months; if a candidate is appointed, then the papers can become part of the individual's personnel file.

For further information, contact the Data Protection Registrar on 01625 545 745.

KNOWING WHAT YOU WANT & GETTING IT RIGHT

SUMMARY: 4 Cs

Compile a job profile.

Create a person profile based on the job profile.

Challenge yourself on the conditions you have listed in the person profile – is that condition really essential? Is that condition relevant to the job tasks? Can you justify the conditions that you have listed?

Check if candidates have any special requirements before you begin your recruitment process to help you consider what reasonable adjustments should be made.

PLANNING THE RECRUITMENT PROCESS

BREAKING IT DOWN INTO STAGES

Having spent time defining the qualities you are looking for, and capturing these in a person profile, the next step is to put in place a process to identify those candidates that best meet this profile.

Spend time at the outset planning:

- **What** needs to happen?
- **When** does it need to happen?
- **Who** needs to be involved?

Most managers and candidates would anticipate that any recruitment event will consist of a series of assessment stages with some candidates proceeding to the next stage and others not. The key is to know:

- What should happen at each stage?
- How many stages should I have?

A SERIES OF FILTERS

View each stage as a series of filters:

- Initial stage(s) of selection
- Second stage of selection
- Final stage of selection

In earlier stages of the process we use our *wide filters* to screen out candidates if they fail to meet certain key criteria, such as educational qualifications, not having particular technical experience, or not holding a full driving licence, etc.

PLANNING THE RECRUITMENT PROCESS

INITIAL STAGE

The initial stage would include tools such as:

- Telephone interviews
- CV or application form sifting

Initial stage tools have not been found to be as accurate as certain other methods of selection when used on their own; the reality being that they are more suited to making broad-brush distinctions between candidates. They still have, however, a valuable role to play when used as part of a wider recruitment process.

They tend to be much more cost-effective than the more expensive methods that are needed later in the process to make finer distinctions between stronger candidates.

SECOND STAGE

Here you will be dealing with fewer candidates. As these candidates have all passed your initial filter, however, they will – as a group – be of better overall quality. Your selection methods therefore need to be capable of making more sophisticated distinctions between candidates.

These methods tend to be more expensive, but you often get what you pay for – the key is getting the most out of them by using them at the right time in the right place.

PLANNING THE RECRUITMENT PROCESS

SECOND STAGE

The tools often used at the second stage include:

- Structured face-to-face interviews exploring each candidate's career history and technical competence/skill
- Psychometric testing (such as verbal and numerical tests pitched at an appropriate level to the role being assessed)
- Work sample exercises (which replicate, as far as possible, certain aspects of the job, eg a welding test for the job of a welder. Work sample exercises are also often used at the **final** stage)

Depending upon the level of the role and other factors, such as likely applicant numbers and timescale, you may decide that the second stage will also be the final stage in the process.

PLANNING THE RECRUITMENT PROCESS

FINAL STAGE

This is where you need to use your better quality (and more expensive) selection methods to make the fine distinctions between the remaining candidates (often termed the short-listed candidates).

Fine-filter selection methods include *multiple event* processes, such as an assessment centre. Assessment centres:

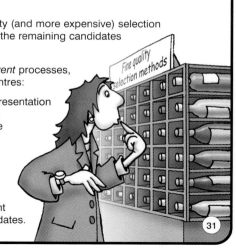

- Use several different selection methods eg presentation exercises, additional interviews, a personality questionnaire, and/or a work sample exercise

- Draw upon several different assessors

- Integrate the results of the exercises in a structured way

- Can last a full day

Some organisations use just one or two different exercises to whittle down the short-list of candidates.

WHO NEEDS TO BE INVOLVED?

The key individuals to involve in any recruitment process are:

Line managers
Line managers are amongst the most important people to be involved in a recruitment process because they will ultimately be managing the appointed candidate on a day-to-day basis.

HR/Personnel
HR/Personnel are a key internal resource for any manager. They will have information on the established recruitment processes used within the organisation and can advise on recruitment law and the relevance/appropriateness of the various methods of selection.

They may also be able to provide expertise in running psychometric assessment or assessment centres.

WHO NEEDS TO BE INVOLVED?

Other managers in the organisation
In addition to line management involvement, another important group of people to consider involving in the process are managers who would have close contact with the role – for example, they could be *internal customers*.

These managers could be:

- Consulted about the qualities that are important for the role
- Be part of the interview processes
- Be involved at the final assessment stage

PLANNING THE RECRUITMENT PROCESS

WHO NEEDS TO BE INVOLVED?

The candidates themselves need to have their say!
Effective selection is a two-way process – candidates need to be involved and to feel engaged by the recruitment process.

This means that they will need sufficient information on the organisation and the role to decide if they feel the job would be right for them.

So, when designing the process, consider:

- What information will the candidates need?
- What will you want them to see (such as where they would actually be working)?
- Who will you want them to meet (such as team members, colleagues and key *internal customers*)?
- How can you provide them with the opportunity to ask any questions that they may have?

WHO NEEDS TO BE INVOLVED?

Team colleagues
It can be invaluable to provide an opportunity for candidates to meet the actual colleagues they would be working with if appointed.

This provides candidates with an opportunity to get a better feel for the organisation, the role, and the actual team of which they would become a part.

Provided that the team members have been appropriately trained, and that the meeting is appropriately structured, the meeting could also feed information into the selection process.

PLANNING THE RECRUITMENT PROCESS

WHO NEEDS TO BE INVOLVED?

External consultants
Another important group you could involve in the process is external consultants.
For example:

- Recruitment consultants putting forward those candidates whom they feel best meet the essential criteria for the role

- Search consultants (sometimes called *head-hunters*) who would be commissioned to identify individuals most suited for the role, and could also assist in the interview process

- Assessment/HR consultants who could design the recruitment process from start to finish and be involved in the delivery of certain stages – such as psychometric assessment or the running of the assessment centres

WHAT SHOULD HAPPEN AT EACH STAGE?

The choice of what should happen at each stage will be driven by a number of factors, including:

- The qualities you are looking for
- The number of candidates you expect to apply – 10, 100 or 1,000
- The number of vacancies you are seeking to fill – 1 or 10
- The available budget – price may eliminate the use of certain methods of selection
- The timescale – this will influence how many times you can ask candidates to come back for assessment
- The recruitment/selection expertise you have available, either internally or from external sources such as consultants. Do you have an internal resource who could undertake psychometric assessment for you or would you need to buy this in from an external consultancy firm?

PLANNING THE RECRUITMENT PROCESS

CAPTURING INFORMATION

Map the person profile against those methods you could use to capture information in each area, remembering to focus on those qualities identified as *essential* during the earlier stages of your recruitment process.

Candidates who fail to meet one of the essential criteria early in the process (for example, not having a driving licence, a particular qualification or whose written communication is poor) will be rejected at that stage.

Aim to capture information against each quality at least twice by the end of the process, to ensure solid measurement for those stronger candidates reaching the final stage.

Certain qualities may need further exploring if they are particularly important for the role or they are potentially more challenging to assess accurately (such as a candidate's technical experience or level of technical skill).

CAPTURING INFORMATION

If you were looking at a field service engineer role, you might look to gather information against the qualities as shown below:

	CV & Additional information	Technical interview	Personality questionnaire	Final structured interview
Experience	✔	✔		
Technical knowledge & skills	✔	✔		✔
Qualifications	✔	✔		
Communication		✔	✔	✔
Teamwork		✔	✔	
Initiative			✔	✔
Flexibility			✔	✔
Drive			✔	✔

PLANNING THE RECRUITMENT PROCESS

CAPTURING INFORMATION

The various stages of gathering information would then consist of:

Step one – Initial information exchange
An application pack will be sent out providing further information on the role and the organisation. This provides candidates with the opportunity to confirm that the role would give them what they are looking for.

The application pack will also include an *additional information* form which candidates will need to complete to ensure that they provide the information needed for the *Step two* assessment.

Step two – CV and additional information form sift
Aspects of the candidates' experience, qualifications – covering areas such as driving licence and relevant technical qualifications – and technical skills/knowledge are objectively assessed.

PLANNING THE RECRUITMENT PROCESS

CAPTURING INFORMATION

Step three – Technical interview/site visit or tour
Measures in greater depth their technical knowledge and
skills, as well as selected competencies such as oral
communication and teamwork.

**Step four – Final structured
interview/personality questionnaire**
Measures the remaining competencies, as
well as capturing further information on
some of the areas already assessed.

PLANNING THE RECRUITMENT PROCESS

SUMMARY

- Your recruitment process should be structured around key, relevant and justifiable qualities
- Ensure it is realistic in light of your timescale, anticipated candidate numbers, available resources and budget
- Initial stage methods are only really suitable for making broad brush distinctions between candidates
- You need more accurate selection methods at the final stages, when it is harder to differentiate between better quality candidates
- Are you involving all the key people you need to in the process?
- Finally, but crucially, remember that selection is a two-way process – candidates also need the opportunity to gather information and to decide if the role would be right for them. As well as being fair and robust, the process needs to look and feel right from the candidate's perspective if it is to succeed

ATTRACTING THE RIGHT CANDIDATES

INTRODUCTION

A key part in any recruitment process is attracting candidates – it just doesn't work without them!

For some larger and higher-profile organisations, attracting large numbers of candidates is not a problem: in fact they will often be swamped with candidates for certain positions. Their challenge is to reduce the numbers of unsuitable candidates applying!

CHALLENGES

For other organisations, attracting any candidates may be a challenge – possibly there will only be a handful of people in the country, or even the world, with the required technical knowledge or expertise.

Alternatively, the issue might be that it is difficult to attract candidates from particular ethnic minority groups, or female applicants or from particular age groups.

There are a number of methods that organisations now have at their disposal when it comes to attracting candidates. However, before reviewing the various options and the benefits/drawbacks of each, be clear about what you are trying to achieve.

ATTRACTING THE RIGHT CANDIDATES

YOUR GOAL

You are seeking someone who meets the person profile and who feels that your organisation is right for them. To ensure that you attract the right people, and dissuade those for whom the role would not be right, you need to:

- Have a very clear and realistic picture of the organisation – its culture, goals and future direction. This needs to be communicated to ensure that the organisation's values match those of any potential candidate
- Have all the information that a candidate will want to know about the organisation, its structure and the specific responsibilities of the role
- Know what is likely to attract someone to the organisation and role (the *upside* of the job), as well as the more negative aspects (the *downside*)
- Communicate clearly to potential candidates what the essential qualities are, drawing upon a detailed understanding of the person profile
- Have a good feel as to where potential applicants will be coming from, so that you can choose the most appropriate strategies to target them

NATIONAL PRESS ADVERTISING

There are many different ways to attract candidates to a particular role, but each method has its benefits and drawbacks. Looking first at advertising, you can consider placing ads in the national, local or trade press.

National press

Benefits

- Can generate a high quality field of candidates
- Has been the traditional recruitment media to use
- Can be used as an opportunity to raise the profile of the organisation externally

Drawbacks

- Can be very costly
- Candidates can be drawn from a national and international field, which may involve the further expense of relocation
- If the candidates miss the advertisement, that's it!

Roll up, Roll up, exciting opportunity on 4th floor

OTHER PRESS ADVERTISING

Local press

Benefits

- Considerably cheaper than national advertising
- The candidate pool is more local
- Raises the organisation's profile locally

Drawbacks

- As with national advertising, it is a single shot method
- The local area may not contain a sufficiently large pool of candidates

Trade press

Benefits

- Often appropriate for more technical or specialist roles
- Prices generally cheaper than national advertising

Drawbacks

- Some technical media have infrequent publication dates
- Depending upon the media and job content, candidate response volumes can be very low

PUTTING TOGETHER A GOOD ADVERT

- Place in a media likely to be reviewed by the target audience. A good recruitment advertising agency should be able to advise on the best media options to use

- Create an accurate picture of the organisation and its culture – in other words, do not describe the culture as fast-paced, entrepreneurial and client-focused if it is not!

- Clearly communicate the core responsibilities of the role and the essential qualities required from prospective candidates

- State 'what's in it for the candidate' – promote the upside of the role but do not over-sell what it can offer. If the salary and benefits package is attractive, include it as a 'selling point'; if it is less attractive, still include it to manage candidates' expectations, but concentrate instead upon the non-financial attractions of the role, such as comprehensive training, or career progression potential

- Be careful that the wording used does not discourage particular groups from applying

- State exactly what interested candidates need to do to apply – email/ send a CV, etc

EXAMPLE RECRUITMENT ADVERT

Territory Sales Executive
Retail Sales OTE £30k plus benefits

Wright Retail is one of the UK's leading specialist sports equipment suppliers with retail outlets across the UK. We pride ourselves on a fun, team orientated approach to providing high quality customer service. Due to continued growth in the business, we have an opportunity for a new Territory Sales Executive to cover the Midlands area.

This is an exciting opportunity for anyone looking to move into a retail sales environment. Reporting to the Regional Sales Manager, the Sales Executive is responsible for maximizing revenue from new and existing accounts.

If you thrive when working in a results-orientated environment, are prepared to take the initiative and are comfortable working remotely in a field sales role, then we would love to hear from you. In addition to good oral and written communication skills, you will have at least 5 GCSE passes, a minimum of 1 year's commercial experience and a full clean current UK driving licence.

If you feel that this is the challenge you are looking for, please forward a CV and covering letter to John Sponton, HR Officer, Wright Retail, Albion Court, 110 Ash Road, Midtown MX1 1XX or email John.Sponton@WrightRetail.com by **Tuesday 16th March 20XX.**

Wright Retail operates a policy of equal opportunities in employment. We select people for jobs without regard to disability, marital status, age, race, gender, religion or sexual orientation.

ATTRACTING THE RIGHT CANDIDATES

CHECKLIST FOR A GOOD ADVERT

Putting together a good advert is about getting on the right TRACK:

Targeted – to candidates qualified for the role through the choice of media

Reflective – of the role and its responsibilities

Attractive – both in its content (eg the description of the financial benefits and non-financial factors) and appearance (its layout and – where budgets allow – graphics/use of colour)

Clear – so that candidates know exactly how to apply

Keeping – focused on what it's there to do – bringing the right candidates in to the start of a selection process

INTERNAL CANDIDATES

Benefits

- Too easily overlooked as a potential candidate pool – they know the organisation better than anyone
- No external advertising costs
- Gives career development opportunities to those within an organisation

Drawbacks

- Depending upon the size of the organisation, it may be hard to find internal candidates who meet the person profile sufficiently. Internal candidates should be assessed in the same way as external candidates
- Creates a vacancy elsewhere in the organisation which has to be filled in its turn

INTERNET JOB SITES

Benefits

- Generally very cheap
- Can be very quick
- The advert stays on for a period, rather than being a once only appearance
- There is a wide range of specialist and generalist job sites available
- Probably the media of choice for certain candidate groups these days, eg recent graduates, IT candidates

Drawbacks

- The volume of response can be extremely variable
- The quality of response can be extremely variable
- Some job sites have a poor reputation for taking jobs off their job boards, meaning you can still be receiving candidate details a long time after the job is filled

YOUR COMPANY WEBSITE

Benefits

- Reduces dependence upon job sites
- Makes best use of a natural source of candidates

Drawbacks

- The initial start up costs
- The investment of time and effort in keeping the website up-to-date, and the systems needed to process and track candidate applications
- Candidate response may be limited unless you are a large employer with a well-known brand

RECRUITMENT AGENCIES & CONSULTANCIES

SUCCESS-ONLY BASIS

Benefits

- You only pay a fee when a person is appointed
- Can be very quick
- Avoids the need for advertising if the post is especially sensitive or confidential

Drawbacks

- The quality of agencies and their service levels is extremely variable
- Agencies tend to place more emphasis upon attracting than selecting (ie you can get a lot of applications to screen and interview!)
- Costs can be high

RECRUITMENT AGENCIES & CONSULTANCIES
RETAINED BASIS

Benefits

- Because you are paying fees up-front and upon a stage-by-stage basis, the quality of service should be, and generally is, better, with greater emphasis upon selection, advice and consultancy

- For very scarce or specialist roles, this is often the only route available

Drawbacks

- Staged costs mean that you can end up having paid a high proportion of the overall fee, but still have been ultimately unsuccessful in filling the post

ATTRACTING THE RIGHT CANDIDATES

RECRUITMENT AGENCIES & CONSULTANCIES
GETTING THE BEST OUT OF THEM

- Ask around for recommendations of good recruitment agencies or consultancies which specialise in the type of role you are recruiting for
- Use a preferred supplier list if one exists within your organisation
- Give a clear brief on the qualities of the candidate you require – some consultants will ask for a meeting or a visit to take the brief in person
- Watch out for hidden costs to the assignment: consultant travel, researcher costs, etc
- Ask to be kept involved in how the assignment is progressing
- Give specific feedback on the quality of the candidates as you review them so the consultant can fine-tune their approach if required
- Establish milestones and timelines for monitoring progress of the consultant/agency

ATTRACTING THE RIGHT CANDIDATES

SUMMARY

- Have a clear picture of the organisation, the role and the sort of person you are looking for

- Ensure a realistic picture of the above is clearly communicated to your potential candidates through whichever method you use

- Know where you are likely to find your target candidate pool and use the most appropriate attraction strategies to target them

- Monitor whichever attraction methods you use so you can fine-tune and refine your recruitment processes in the future

ASSESSING CVs &
APPLICATION FORMS

ASSESSING CVs & APPLICATION FORMS

INTRODUCTION

Screening candidates' applications fairly and objectively will ensure that only suitable candidates are invited to interview.

Candidates' applications usually take the form of:

- A CV, or Curriculum Vitae – meaning literally, 'the course of life'
- A traditional hand-written or typed application form
- A hybrid online application form/CV created by a career jobsite on the internet

Each format has its strengths and weaknesses. Consider these before deciding which method you wish to use for your next piece of recruitment.

CV-BASED APPLICATIONS

CV-based applications are often accompanied by a covering letter.

Benefits

- The layout, quality, length and presentation of a CV and covering letter can give interesting insights into a candidate's personality style and communication skills

- From a candidate perspective, this is one of the most acceptable ways of applying for a job

Drawbacks

- For the same reasons, CVs vary wildly in quality and length and it can be difficult to access the key information you need

- It is easy for candidates to omit information which they might prefer not to expose, such as gaps in their employment history

TRADITIONAL APPLICATION FORMS

Benefits

- Application forms ensure that candidates give you the information you want in a consistent and structured way

- The investment of time and effort required to complete an application form is itself a sign of the candidate's interest and commitment in applying for your role

Drawbacks

- It takes time to design your own application form

- Candidates find completing application forms tiresome – it can put off some good candidates from applying altogether

ONLINE APPLICATION FORMS

Benefits

- Online application documents can be sifted and stored electronically

- Candidates find this a quick, easy and effective way to apply for jobs

- Software is available which can score certain online application forms quickly and accurately

Drawbacks

- The quality, and content, of online application forms can vary wildly

DESIGNING YOUR OWN FORM

If you decide to design your own application form, include:

- Personal details eg address and contact information (but avoid questions which are unnecessary, cannot be justified, or could be construed as discriminatory, such as 'personal circumstances')

- Details of current or most recent employment, including dates and responsibilities held

- Details of previous employment

- Education and professional qualifications

- Questions which gather information about relevant competencies

- Any other information the individual feels is relevant, eg specific work experience, experience gained from extra-curricular hobbies or interests, etc

- References, with a clear note of when and how these will be taken up (eg after offer)

- A detachable sheet, not containing the person's name, asking for information for equal opportunities monitoring. (See next page)

And finally:

- Avoid asking for an accompanying photo

- Keep to a maximum of 4 or 5 A4 pages

ASSESSING CVs & APPLICATION FORMS

EQUAL OPPORTUNITIES FORM

EXAMPLE

ABC Ltd operates a policy of equal opportunities in employment. We select people for jobs without regard to disability, marital status, age, race, gender, religion or sexual orientation. To enable us to monitor this policy, please answer the following questions. The following information will be treated as strictly confidential **and will be used for equal opportunities monitoring purposes only.**

AGE:_____ GENDER: M/F_____ MARITAL STATUS: Single/Engaged/Married/Separated/Divorced

I would describe my ethnic origin as follows (please tick box):

White	White British	❏	White Irish	❏
Mixed Race	White and Black Caribbean	❏	White and Black African	❏
	White and Asian	❏		
Chinese	Chinese	❏		
Black/Black British	Caribbean	❏	African	❏
Asian/Asian British	Indian	❏	Pakistani	❏
	Bangladeshi	❏		
Other	Please specify:			

Do you have a disability you would like us to know about?   YES/NO
If YES, briefly describe the nature of the disability so we know how we can help you:

GETTING INFORMATION FROM APPLICATION DOCUMENTS

A key component of fair and effective recruitment is the paper screening stage.

The most common traps to fall into when assessing applications are:

- Not being clear what you are looking for
- Treating a candidate more favourably because they remind you of yourself – similar education, background, experiences, etc
- Not spending enough quality time on the paper screening stage
- Being put off by the first impression of their application
- Assessing applications inconsistently
- Being influenced, negatively or positively, by their handwriting

GETTING INFORMATION FROM APPLICATION DOCUMENTS

Help to improve your objectivity by designing and using a simple tick-box style form – an application screening form, linked to the person profile *(see Knowing what you want & getting it right)*.

Keep the form:

- Simple and easy to use

- Relevant to the person profile

- Based **only** upon criteria which can be clearly identified or inferred from a candidate's application documents

Then allow sufficient time, space and freedom from distractions to assess the candidates' applications properly. Ideally, work with a colleague who can check the scoring.

Look at the example overleaf for an imaginary sales manager job selling paints to big DIY retailers.

ASSESSING CVs & APPLICATION FORMS

SALES MANAGER APPLICATION SCREENING FORM

Candidate name: **Reference number:**

	Ideal	Acceptable	Questionable	Reject
Higher Qualifications	Masters, Degree, or HND	HNC	Not known	Less than HNC
Basic Qualifications*	GCSE Maths and English, above C pass	GCSE Maths and English, C pass	Not known	No GCSE Maths and English
Experience selling to large retailers	Yes, over 5 years	Yes, 2–5 years	Yes, but under 2 years	None
Driving licence	Yes, clean or under 6 points	Yes, but 6–9 points	Not known	Not got/lost
Range of experience gained (based on below)	All/most	Some	Few	None

* Other qualifications equivalent to GCSE could include O Levels, ONC/OND in relevant subjects.

Range of experience gained:
How many of the following areas has the candidate clearly stated, or can reasonably be inferred, from the CV/Application Form and covering letter? (please tick):

Negotiation ☐   Trade and product knowledge ☐   IT skills ☐

OVERALL RECOMMENDATION:

Proceed to interview ☐

Hold ☐   Reject ☐

COMMUNICATING PROFESSIONALLY WITH ALL CANDIDATES

It is essential:

✔ To retain the interest and enthusiasm of the short-listed candidates

✔ To pass on the bad news to the unsuccessful candidates in a professional and sensitive manner

You want to keep your short-listed candidates positive and focused, and you don't want your rejected candidates to feel, well, rejected. When rejecting candidates, remember:

✗ Unsuccessful candidates today could be your customers tomorrow!

✗ Your good name could be bad-mouthed to your suppliers, customers and competitors!

✗ Unsuccessful candidates may well be potentially successful candidates for other roles in the future

✗ How you felt last time you were rejected by an employer

Look at the final chapter for how to handle unsuccessful candidates with sensitivity.

ASSESSING CVs & APPLICATION FORMS

SUMMARY

- Use documents which will gather the right amount and quality of information

- Assess the application documents fairly and objectively, based upon the role's person profile – give this the time and effort it deserves

- Communicate promptly and professionally with your candidates, whether they were successful at the first stage or not

MAKING THE
INTERVIEW WORK

MAKING THE INTERVIEW WORK

INTRODUCTION

Interviews are still one of the most popular methods of selection:

- 99% of companies use interviews
- They can be cost-effective if done well
- They fulfil a psychological need to meet and see a person who might one day join the organisation
- When conducted effectively, interviews can accurately predict job performance

However, there are key pitfalls to be avoided. An interview delivered without structure and planning rapidly **loses** its ability to predict good performers.

There are different types of interview, each providing quite specific types of information:

- Biographical interview
- Situational interview
- Competency or behavioural interview
- Technical interview

BIOGRAPHICAL INTERVIEW

This type of interview explores a candidate's past experiences in a chronological way.

Two sample questions:

'Why did you move from job xx to job yy?'
'What were you doing between…. and …..?'

Good for:

- Exploring the reasons why a candidate's career has progressed in the way it has and why they have made important career moves or choices

- Clarifying a candidate's work experience, knowledge and qualifications

TECHNICAL INTERVIEW

This interview explores a candidate's technical knowledge, qualifications, experience and skills.

Two sample questions:

'What project management techniques have you used?'

'What would you use component/system x for?'

Good for:

- Exploring whether a candidate is capable of performing the job to the desired technical level or what training or support they might require if appointed

COMPETENCY OR BEHAVIOURAL INTERVIEW

The competency interview is used to explore a candidate's particular behaviours or abilities.

The following question relates to the competency of team working (*see page 17*):

'Tell me about a time you helped out some colleagues who were facing a particularly difficult problem.'

Depending upon the candidate's response, some useful follow-up (called 'probing') questions are:

- *'What part did you play specifically?'*
- *'What happened next?'*
- *'What was the final outcome?'*

> **Top Tip**
> Have a couple of opening questions prepared in order to fully explore a competency area.

Good for:

- Exploring how a person's skills, gained from handling situations in the past, would transfer to your job

MAKING THE INTERVIEW WORK

SITUATIONAL INTERVIEW

In situational interviews, you ask hypothetically-based questions, exploring how someone might do a job if appointed.

This question could be used when recruiting for a manager of a shop:

'A customer has just rung in, very angrily complaining about the service they received from one of your sales staff. What steps would you take?'

Good for:

- Exploring how a person might do a job: this can be useful when their experience is relatively 'untried' in that particular area
- Seeing how a candidate's **existing** knowledge or experience could be applied to handle **future** issues or problems

There is a danger with these sort of questions that a candidate may answer in a theoretical way – rather than what they would really do. If in doubt, use competency/behavioural interview questions alongside situational questions to explore how they **have** actually dealt with related situations in the past.

SEQUENCE & FORMAT

Give thought to the **best sequence** and **format** of interviews as well as the types of questions.

Top tips for the best interview sequence:

- Establish your candidates' technical abilities before concentrating upon the more complex process of assessing their competencies and fit within your organisation

- Telephone-based or webcam-based interviews can be very effective in particular circumstances, for example when your candidates are widely spread geographically

SEQUENCE & FORMAT

Top tips for the best interview format:

- Individual (one on one) interviews allow for greater rapport with a candidate *but* have potential for greater interviewer bias

- Panel (multiple interviewer) interviews can be fairer *but* are harder to manage and can be very formal and intimidating for candidates

- Telephone-based interviews can avoid travel challenges for candidates and interviewers alike, *but* it is harder to build rapport

Whichever sequence or format you use, it is important to be consistent. Do not, for example, start with face-to-face interviews for some, and then switch to telephone interviews halfway through the process.

KEY INTERVIEWING SKILLS

'N, O, P, Q, R, S, T, U'

N – Note taking	**Take notes** or you will forget information and not have a record to support your decisions.
O – Objectives	**Know what you are looking for** from the candidate (experience, knowledge, skills, competencies).
P – Preparation	**Prepare** – analyse the job, plan your interview, book the room, review your paperwork.
Q – Questions	**Ask good questions** – *open* (to open up an area), *probing* (to explore an area further), *closed* (to confirm facts), *targeted* (tailored to key areas).

Adapted from a mnemonic quoted in *Competency Based Recruitment and Selection*, by Robert Wood and Tim Payne (Wiley, 1998)

KEY INTERVIEWING SKILLS

'N, O, P, Q, R, S, T, U'

R – Rapport	**Establish rapport** so you get the best out of each candidate and get an accurate insight into how they typically behave.
S – Structure	**Follow a structure** that ensures you cover the areas you need to, and that gives the candidate a chance to ask questions.
T – Time management	**Make effective use of time** and stick to your allocated time.
U – Unbiased	Be aware of your biases – your pet likes and pet hates. Make a clear and conscious effort to stop them influencing your decision making.

CONDUCTING THE INTERVIEW PROFESSIONALLY

- Start on time and welcome the candidate
- Introduce yourself and explain the interview and recruitment process
- Provide an overview of the organisation and the role
- Keep a written reminder of the questions you have prepared, and stick to them
- Avoid sitting behind a desk and adopting confrontational body language – the best interviews are conducted professionally but informally
- Listen politely and show interest in the candidate's responses but avoid showing specific approval or disapproval of what they say
- Summarise to check your understanding of key points
- Ask good questions and take good notes – see below
- Manage the time to ensure you cover all the questions you need
- Ask the candidates if they have any questions – remember it is a two-way process
- Conclude by thanking the candidate for their time and interest in your role and advise them when they will hear about the outcome

MAKING THE INTERVIEW WORK

ASKING GOOD QUESTIONS

This is all about:

- Knowing what you are looking for
- Planning and writing down your questions in advance
- Asking the right types of questions to get you there

In the interview itself, think about **TOFFEE**:

- Take the **T**ime that the interview needs
- Be organised so as to reach your **O**bjectives
- **F**ind out the **F**acts
- Offer **E**ncouragement for **E**xamples

'I try not to miss a thing'

MAKING THE INTERVIEW WORK

ASKING GOOD QUESTIONS

Useful questions to use include:

Open – Starts an area for the interview to explore and encourages the candidate to provide further information:

'Tell me about…', *'Give me an example of….'*
'Who – ?', *'What – ?'*, *'Where – ?'*, *'When – ?'*, *'Why – ?'*

Probing – Use to 'dig' under the candidate's responses and explore an area:

'What happened next?', *'How did you deal with…?'*

Closed – Can be used selectively to clarify specific information and control the interview. They can often lead to a simple 'yes' or 'no' response:

'Did you…?', *'Have you ever…?'*, *'Who did you report to?'*

ASKING GOOD QUESTIONS

Avoid:

 Too many closed questions

 Leading questions suggesting that your mind is made up – *'Surely that was not a sensible decision?'*

 Forced multiple choice questions – *'So was the problem caused by x, y, or z?'*

 'Marathon runner' questions – questions that go on and on and on…

TAKING GOOD NOTES

✔ Record as much factual evidence as possible by jotting down notes – do not use electronic recording devices as this can be intimidating, and would be unethical if used without the candidate's permission

✔ Record non-verbal behaviour in your notes, but do so objectively

✔ Concentrate on asking the right questions and recording the candidate's responses **during** the interview – then assess the responses **after** the interview is finished

Taking notes during the interview is essential to ensure that the recruitment decision is as fair and objective as possible; it will provide a record in case your decision is challenged.

MAKING THE INTERVIEW WORK

EVALUATING THE RESULTS

When ?

● After the interview has finished and the candidate has left the room, while the interview is still fresh in your mind

How ?

● Start from the beginning of your interview notes, and go through each piece of evidence that you recorded. This evidence could be what was described **to** you **by** the candidate or what was observed **by** you **about** the candidate

● Relate the evidence to the job and person profile criteria by using ticks and crosses

● Remember that some of the evidence you noted may relate to more than one criterion or competency

● Omission of behaviour could also be important (negative) evidence, such as not responding to a question

EVALUATING THE RESULTS

Guard against your own biases, pet likes or dislikes, or subjective opinions when evaluating interview performance.

Weigh up both the quality and the quantity of evidence you have gathered in each of the areas of interest, based upon the pattern and volume of ticks and crosses you have given.

To help you with this, use a rating scale as shown overleaf.

EVALUATING THE RESULTS

Rating	Description
5 Exceptional	Meets all or virtually all of the competency description – no significant omissions.
4 Good	Meets most of the competency description; many indicators observed in full and others partially; any omissions or negative areas were not critical to the overall performance in this area.
3 Acceptable	Meets more than half of the competency description – is capable of performing at the level required; some negative evidence observed.
2 Some weakness	Meets less than half the competency description; some critical positive indicators omitted; more negative areas/evidence observed.
1 Poor	Meets almost none of the competency description; very little positive evidence observed; outweighed by negative indicators.
0 No evidence	No evidence shown when given an opportunity to demonstrate the competency.

SECOND INTERVIEWS

- Use your objective assessment of the candidates' first interview ratings to decide whom to invite back for second interview or further assessment

- Second interviews should use exactly the same techniques as already outlined above, but should be used for focusing upon specific areas outstanding from the selection process so far, or upon concerns raised during the first interview which require clarification

- Do not just repeat the questions covered in the first interview – think of alternative questions designed to explore more fully the areas that you need to cover

MAKING THE INTERVIEW WORK

SUMMARY

- Plan the sequence and format of the interviews to best suit your recruitment requirement and available resources

- Decide what you want to cover in each interview, linked to the job and person profile

- Generate beforehand the interview questions that will get you that information

- Ask good questions and take good notes

- Evaluate the candidates' responses fairly and objectively, as soon as possible after the interview has concluded

OTHER SELECTION METHODS

ACCURACY OF DIFFERENT METHODS

Some methods are more accurate than others when it comes to gathering information on different knowledge and competency areas. Occupational psychologists* have statistically analysed just how accurate different methods of selection are.

Research has shown:

- No one method of selection is perfect at predicting actual performance of a person in a job

- By combining different methods, however, the chances of getting it right are increased

- Some methods, such as graphology (the study of handwriting) and phrenology (the study of the shape of the head) are little better than a random method, such as tossing a coin, at predicting a candidate's behaviour!

* Mike Smith et al 2001

OTHER SELECTION METHODS

TYPES OF EXERCISE

Well designed, well managed methods which have better records of predicting performance include:

- Work sample exercises
- Psychometric tests and personality questionnaires
- Presentation exercises
- Group discussion exercises and practical group exercises

Top tips

- Use different methods of selection, alongside interviewing, to get a fuller and more rounded picture of your candidates' abilities
- Use the results carefully, alongside the results of other parts of the recruitment process
- Stick to methods which have proven track records

OTHER SELECTION METHODS

WORK SAMPLE EXERCISES

These exercises aim to replicate aspects of the job in as realistic a way as possible.

Flight simulators used for experienced aircraft pilot recruitment, or a timed assembly task, using small components, for a production line operator involved in the manufacture of electrical goods, are examples of work sample tests.

Advantages

- Gives the candidate a valuable insight into the role through the *realism* of the exercise
- Can be a very effective selection tool if properly used

Disadvantages

- Can be difficult and time-consuming to design
- Can be expensive to buy in and to run

WORK SAMPLE EXERCISES

Top tips for using work sample tests or exercises:

- Consider key aspects or tasks relating to the job in question, and how these could be replicated in a practical task for the candidate to carry out

- Contact a reputable test publisher to see if good off-the-shelf exercises can be purchased

- If designing your own exercise, make sure the instructions are clear and the exercise falls within the level of knowledge, experience or competence required for the job. Test it out on a willing colleague beforehand!

OTHER SELECTION METHODS

PSYCHOMETRIC TESTS & PERSONALITY QUESTIONNAIRES

Psychometric means literally 'measurement of the mind'.

These sorts of exercises provide objective measures on candidates' aptitudes, abilities or preferred ways of working by statistically comparing their responses to large, representative sample groups.

Advantages

- Can be very effective selection tools if properly used
- Can often be fairer and more objective than interviewing on its own
- Relatively cheap to run, once the relevant training and materials are in place
- Increasingly available to use online

Disadvantages

- The better quality psychometric exercises require expensive and time-consuming training and materials to get up and running

OTHER SELECTION METHODS

PSYCHOMETRIC TESTS & PERSONALITY QUESTIONNAIRES

Top tips for using psychometric exercises:

- Do not consider designing your own – this requires highly specialist knowledge

- Be wary of poorer quality psychometric exercises which exist in abundance in the marketplace. Before buying and using psychometric exercises, seek advice from reputable independent sources, such as the British Psychological Society (0116 254 9568)

- Consider using experienced and trained consultants who specialise in the professional application and interpretation of these powerful exercises

- Ensure you give good feedback to candidates

PRESENTATION EXERCISES

These can be used to assess a candidate's communication skills, and if relevant, technical knowledge.

Advantages
- Relatively easy to design, use and incorporate into an assessment day
- A good way of involving colleagues as assessors

Disadvantages
- Not all candidates present well, but may be good at other aspects of the job – so keep the results in proportion

Top tips for using presentation exercises:
- The topic should be clear and not too complicated – *how/what/where/when/why* are good opening words to use
- The topic can be given either on the day, or in advance, but you must be consistent between the candidates and they should be clearly briefed. Both approaches yield different types of relevant information. For candidates asked to prepare in advance, the varying amounts of preparation invested can be illuminating. For candidates preparing on the day, you have an ideal opportunity to see how they perform on a level playing field, with limited (equal) time

OTHER SELECTION METHODS

OTHER COMMONLY USED EXERCISES

Other types of exercise to consider are:

- Group discussion exercises – getting the candidates to resolve a series of problems around a table through discussion and negotiation

- Practical group exercises – getting the candidates to work together to solve a problem using practical resource materials, such as large construction kits

- Role play exercises – simulating an important aspect of the role such as a meeting with a member of staff to resolve a work-related problem

- In-tray exercises (also called in-basket exercises) – aiming to replicate the 'in tray' of the post in question; these are often in the form of an assorted collection of emails, notes and briefing information containing problems or issues to be tackled

TECHNICAL ASSESSMENT

Technical assessment exercises are used to assess a candidate's existing technical knowledge, skills and experience.

Advantages

- Technical assessment can be achieved in different ways through a specially designed interview, a presentation, or a work sample exercise

Disadvantages

- You need to ensure that it is fair and relevant to the post. Pay particular attention to the use of any in-house jargon or terminology in problems you set, which may be unfamiliar to an external candidate, or unfairly advantage an internal candidate

Top tips for effective technical assessment:

- Run the chosen exercise past colleagues, particularly those doing the job at the same level – use their results as a benchmark to assess candidates' performance

- Do not place unjustifiable weight on either a better-than-expected or worse-than-expected result – if the latter, keep an open mind about what can be trained. Base your decision fairly and squarely upon the *essential* and *desirable* aspects of the person profile

OTHER SELECTION METHODS

ASSESSMENT CENTRES

Assessment centres combine the results of different types of exercises to form a well-rounded picture of a candidate's attributes and abilities.

They are based around a number of job-relevant competencies, and often place an emphasis upon work sample exercises.

Advantages

- Can be one of the fairest and most thorough ways of assessing candidates
- Provide powerful examples of how a candidate is likely to behave and perform if appointed to the role

Disadvantages

- They are time-consuming to organise and labour-intensive to run
- Candidates need to give up at least half a day to attend the event – many centres last a full day or sometimes longer

OTHER SELECTION METHODS

ASSESSMENT CENTRES

Top tips for using assessment centres:

- Pay particular attention to the timetable on the day so you are not over-committing your candidates and your assessors

- Concentrate the assessment centre on those candidates who have successfully completed the initial selection stages for the role, to make best use of the investment of time needed

- Make sure the assessors are well-briefed so that they can assess the candidates fairly and objectively

- Use different **assessors** across **different** exercises to have different perspectives on each candidate

OTHER SELECTION METHODS

GENERAL GUIDELINES

Whatever additional assessment tests or exercises you use, follow these general principles:

- Tell the candidates in advance what they can expect, so that they have the opportunity to advise you of any special requirements

- Use exercises which are fair and can be assessed consistently and objectively

- Make sure that the exercises are relevant to the person profile

- Integrate the results of each exercise with the other information you have gathered about the candidate, before making a balanced final decision

OTHER SELECTION METHODS

SUMMARY

- Some exercises are better than others for gathering information
- Using different types of well-chosen exercises together does improve your chances of finding the right candidate
- Make sure that any additional exercises you use link to the requirements of the person profile
- Make sure that instructions are clearly explained to the candidate
- It is essential that exercises are objectively scored and assessed
- Weigh up all the candidate's strengths and weaknesses from all of the exercises against the person profile – be fair and balanced when you make your final decisions on a candidate's suitability. See the next chapter for further advice on how to do this

FINAL CHECKS &
MAKING OFFERS

IMPORTANCE OF THE FINAL DECISION

One of the most important parts of the selection process is pulling the information together and ultimately arriving at a decision on a candidate's suitability.

Often the *pulling together* process is carried out immediately after the final assessment stage, just after the candidates have departed.

ASSESSMENT GRIDS

In *Planning the Recruitment Process* we showed how a grid format can be used to plan which exercises can elicit information on particular competencies and skill areas. A similar format can be used to capture how each individual candidate has performed across the relevant areas.

By using an objective rating scale applied across the exercises (see *Making the Interview Work*, for an example), a candidate assessment grid can be created. This can then be reviewed at the end of the selection process with the individual assessors/managers expanding on the ratings given.

A consensus is then reached on each candidate's overall performance against the criteria, and ultimately their suitability for the role.

FINAL CHECKS & MAKING OFFERS

ASSESSMENT GRIDS

EXAMPLE: FIELD SERVICE ENGINEER

	CV & additional information	Technical interview	Personality questionnaire	Final structured interview	Average for criteria
Experience	4	4			4
Technical knowledge & skills	3	4		2	3
Qualifications	3	3			3
Communication		4	✔	3	3.5
Teamwork		4	✔	3	3.5
Initiative			✔	4	4
Flexibility			✔	3	3
Drive			✔	5	5
Overall total against criteria					29 total

Key: 5 – Exceptional, 4 – Good, 3 – Acceptable, 2 – Some weakness, 1 – Poor, 0 – No evidence
Note that personality questionnaires do not usually produce numerical ratings, but rather provide additional information to feed into the decision making process

COMMON PITFALLS

These are some of the common pitfalls which interfere with the pulling together process operating as fairly and as thoroughly as it should:

- Assessors submit partial or incomplete notes which do not sufficiently justify particular ratings
- Gut feelings or other evidence outside of the person profile are allowed to influence the selection decision unjustifiably
- Assessors can often feel by the end of an assessment day that they are as tired as the candidates – there is then a temptation to rush the process or to cut corners
- A balanced and objective perspective on a candidate's overall performance is jeopardised by his/her performance on one particular exercise
- At the other end of the scale, exceptional performance on one exercise means a blind eye is turned to lower performance on other exercises

PULLING SELECTION INFORMATION TOGETHER

- Allow quality time to review the evidence on each candidate
- Base your ratings only upon factual or observed evidence
- Base your assessment upon the person profile criteria
- Consider weighting the criteria to reflect relative importance
- Submit comprehensive and objective notes justifying your ratings on the assessment paperwork
- Have the review process while the information is fresh, but balance this with the need to do it justice

FINAL CHECKS & MAKING OFFERS

MAKING AN OFFER

It is often advisable not to reject your short-listed candidates (or at least your second closest front runner) until your preferred candidate has accepted your offer.

Key points when making an offer:

- There is no binding contract of employment until an offer has been accepted by a candidate on the terms that it was offered

- The offer (and acceptance) can be oral or in writing (including electronic communication)

- Offers can be conditional and subject to factors such as satisfactory references, work permits or a medical

FINAL CHECKS & MAKING OFFERS

CHECKLIST

- Make the offer as quickly as possible – good candidates tend not to hang around

- Consider telephoning the successful candidate to make an offer and invite a preliminary acceptance – this will hopefully avoid you losing your preferred candidate

- Personalise your written offer – start the letter with, *'I'm pleased to be able to confirm...'*, end with *'looking forward to working with you...'*, etc

- Make the package clear – make sure the candidate is fully informed about the full range of benefits on offer

- Invite them to discuss any questions or queries they might have

- Make it easy to accept – enclose a reply paid envelope and duplicate of the offer for the candidate to sign as confirmation

THE IMPORTANCE OF REFERENCE CHECKING

Research has shown that a high proportion of people will look to misrepresent information about themselves when seeking employment.

It is critical to use references to confirm the key historical facts presented during the recruitment process, for instance:

- Do they actually have that qualification?

- Did they actually hold that position for three years?

WHEN TO TAKE UP REFERENCES

When making an offer of employment, it is advisable to make that offer 'subject to satisfactory references being taken up and reviewed'.

Sometimes references may be taken up on all short-listed candidates – an approach more common in the public sector.

It is always important to make candidates aware at the outset when and by what means references will be taken up. This will not only protect against potential issues such as breach of confidentiality, but could also encourage candidates to be more accurate with the information they provide.

TYPES OF REFERENCE

Some of the main types of references that could be sought are:

- Schools, colleges, universities and examination boards
- Written references from previous employers
- Telephone references from employers
- Personal or character references

yes, I can confirm that my son is a lovely lad, ...

Personal or character references tend to be less widely used – often on the grounds that someone is unlikely to suggest a referee who would say anything less than positive about them! However, if they are to be used, it is important to give the referee a clear structure for the areas that you would value comment on.

115

FINAL CHECKS & MAKING OFFERS

FORMAT OF REFERENCES

Written references are always preferable in that they provide a document trail should any issues arise with the appointment in the future. However, telephone references can serve a useful purpose in either confirming a professional/educational qualification or following up on an area of ambiguity arising from a written reference.

An employer has a legal obligation to ensure the fairness and accuracy of any reference provided on a current or former employee. However, an organisation may well only provide the most basic factual information (as shown below) and in some cases company policy could be that they do not provide any references at all:

- Name
- Date of start of employment
- Date of leaving

- Reason for leaving
- Salary details
- Job title

THE RIGHT INFORMATION

When asking for a reference, either over the telephone or in writing, act **FAST**:

Focus on verifiable, factual information (job title, how long in the role, responsibilities, number of direct/indirect reports, budget accountable for, etc).

Ask questions directly related to the person profile for the role.

Seek more than one reference for each candidate.

Treat non-factual information with a healthy degree of scepticism and use it with care.

FINAL CHECKS & MAKING OFFERS

USING MEDICALS

Medical examinations are often used by employers:

- To assess if a candidate is physically capable of performing the role
- To identify the likelihood of sickness absence or injury
- To provide further insight as to how a job may be adjusted to accommodate the special requirements of a potential applicant

Many organisations choose not to hold a medical examination. This is often due to:

- The costs involved
- The extra time required for the examination (which would prolong the recruitment process)
- The fact that, for a lot of roles, physical attributes are not critical criteria

FINAL CHECKS & MAKING OFFERS

USING MEDICALS

A halfway house for many organisations is to use a short medical screening questionnaire at the pre-employment stage.

A fuller medical examination should be sought if there were a concern that a health issue might prove a factor in a person's ability to perform the role or if the nature of the role could impact negatively on their health.

However, there are some roles where a full medical would be an **essential** part of the process for all candidates:

- The uniformed services (fire and rescue, police, etc)
- The armed forces
- Certain security roles
- Roles requiring critical and specific physical/mental attributes (eg air traffic controllers)

HANDLING UNSUCCESSFUL CANDIDATES PROFESSIONALLY

For most organisations, it is important that a professional image is presented of the recruitment process from start to finish. We operate in a small world where candidates are often also potential customers, and people commonly discuss their *experience* of a recruitment process with friends, peers, relatives, suppliers, etc.

As a minimum, you should provide unsuccessful candidates with the following:

- Prompt notification of the final outcome

- A personalised letter, sensitively phrased, acknowledging the time and effort they have invested in the process, and thanking them for their interest in the role/organisation

- An offer to keep their details on file, but only if there is really a chance of a future role – do not raise expectations unnecessarily

- A named contact who could offer comprehensive, objective and relevant feedback on their assessment performance, should they wish for more information

- Sensible suggestions, when giving feedback, for what could improve their chances next time

FINAL CHECKS & MAKING OFFERS

OFF TO A FLYING START

The information you have gathered during recruitment can also be used to help the early training and development of the successful candidate(s) within the organisation.

The early induction of new employees into the organisation is:

The final part of a successful recruitment process.

The first part of a successful retention programme.

Formal responsibility for employee induction normally falls under the remit of HR/Personnel in conjunction with the relevant line manager.

However, even before the candidate starts their employment, there are things that can be done to help them feel motivated and excited about their new job, and to help them hit the ground running on their first day.

OFF TO A FLYING START

- Keep in contact with your successful candidate(s) at an informal level so they don't feel forgotten about – particularly if they are serving a notice period of several months

- Add them to any internal mailing lists for newsletters/company updates

- Forward any corporate materials (brochures/web links/video/DVD) that may be of interest

- Make sure they receive all the necessary personnel documentation (contract of employment, etc) and are clear on the start date and the logistics for their first week

- Make them aware that they can approach you if they have any questions in advance of their start date and formal induction to the organisation

REVIEWING THE PROCESS

The final step in any process is the review. As the phrase goes – 'the proof of the pudding is in the eating'. In some organisations, sufficient numbers of candidates (often 50+) will have been recruited to enable statistical reviews (often termed validation projects) to be made, relating performance on assessments to subsequent actual performance in role.

However, even if large numbers of recruits are not available to conduct full-blown validation projects, there are still a number of measures to look at to gauge the effectiveness/professionalism of the recruitment process:

- On an individual basis, tracking manager evaluations of appointed candidates at key milestones (at end of probation; annual performance reviews) and relating judgments made at the recruitment stages to their actual performance
- Seeking feedback from successful and unsuccessful candidates on how they found the process and their suggestions for improvement
- Seeking feedback and suggestions for improvement from managers involved in the process and from any agencies/consultants involved

REVIEWING THE PROCESS

In addition, useful measures to evaluate the efficiency of a recruitment process would include:

- Identifying the average length of time taken to fill the vacancy

- Calculating the number starting employment divided by the number still employed after 12 months (for multiple recruitment): the closer to one, the better!

- Calculating the direct cost of recruitment and selection per vacancy incurred, such as advertising costs, recruitment agency costs, etc.

- Calculating the indirect costs of recruitment incurred, eg management time spent on running the process

Reviewing your recruitment process is vital. Such reviews could lead you to explore particular areas of your process (how realistic a picture of the job was created; the quality of your interviewers), or it could lead you to sleep more comfortably knowing that the time and effort you invested in getting it right were well spent!

FINAL CHECKS & MAKING OFFERS

SUMMARY

- Make time to review all the information on each of the short-listed candidates before reaching a final decision

- Objectively review the information against the qualities highlighted on the person profile

- Take up references on the successful candidate(s) and seek to verify the key factual information provided during the recruitment process

- Handle the unsuccessful candidates professionally and ensure all are offered feedback on their performance

- Keep in contact with the appointed candidate(s) between offer and start date to ensure their interest and motivation in joining the organisation remain high

- At the end of the recruitment process, undertake a review with the key parties to ascertain what went well and what could be done better next time

successful recruitment – job well done

About the Authors

John Sponton BSc Hons, PgDip, MSc, MCIPD, C.Psychol is a Chartered Occupational Psychologist and a Director of Informed Assessment Ltd. His early career was in HR before working for a leading psychometric test publisher. John then spent a number of years working for the Business Psychology arm of an international HR consultancy, undertaking a wide range of assessment, development, career management and outplacement projects alongside an internal secondment to the HR department.

Stewart Wright BA Hons is a Director of Informed Assessment Ltd. Stewart worked initially in the recruitment industry, gaining a thorough background in recruitment and selection, before specializing in career management, assessment and development for an international HR consultancy. Stewart's practical experience includes the design and validation of selection processes, the design and delivery of recruitment related training workshops, selection exercise design, psychometric assessment and assessment centre management.

ORDER FORM

Your details

Name _____

Position _____

Company _____

Address _____

_____

_____

Telephone _____

Fax _____

E-mail _____

VAT No. (EC companies) _____

Your Order Ref _____

Please send me:

		No. copies
The Managing Recruitment Pocketbook		
The _____ Pocketbook		
The _____ Pocketbook		
The _____ Pocketbook		
The _____ Pocketbook		

Order by Post

MANAGEMENT POCKETBOOKS LTD
LAUREL HOUSE, STATION APPROACH, ALRESFORD,
HAMPSHIRE SO24 9JH UK

Order by Phone, Fax or Internet

Telephone: +44 (0)1962 735573
Facsimile: +44 (0)1962 733637
E-mail: sales@pocketbook.co.uk
Web: www.pocketbook.co.uk

Customers in USA should contact:
Stylus Publishing, LLC, 22883 Quicksilver Drive,
Sterling, VA 20166-2012
Telephone: 703 661 1581 or 800 232 0223
Facsimile: 703 661 1501 E-mail: styluspub@aol.com

THE MANAGEMENT POCKETBOOK SERIES

Pocketbooks

Appraisals
Assertiveness
Balance Sheet
Business Planning
Business Writing
Call Centre Customer Care
Career Transition
Challengers
Coaching
Communicator's
Competencies
Controlling Absenteeism
Creative Manager's
C.R.M.
Cross-cultural Business
Cultural Gaffes
Customer Service
Decision-making
Developing People
Discipline
Diversity
E-commerce
Emotional Intelligence
Employment Law

Empowerment
Energy and Well-being
Facilitator's
Flexible Workplace
Handling Complaints
Icebreakers
Impact & Presence
Improving Efficiency
Improving Profitability
Induction
Influencing
International Trade
Interviewer's
I.T. Trainer's
Key Account Manager's
Leadership
Learner's
Manager's
Managing Budgets
Managing Cashflow
Managing Change
Managing Recruitment
Managing Upwards
Managing Your Appraisal

Marketing
Meetings
Mentoring
Motivation
Negotiator's
Networking
NLP
Openers & Closers
People Manager's
Performance Management
Personal Success
Positive Mental Attitude
Presentations
Problem Behaviour
Problem Solving
Project Management
Quality
Resolving Conflict
Sales Excellence
Salesperson's
Self-managed Development
Starting In Management
Strategy
Stress

Succeeding at Interviews
Teamworking
Telephone Skills
Telesales
Thinker's
Time Management
Trainer Standards
Trainer's
Training Evaluation
Training Needs Analysis
Vocal Skills

Pocketsquares

Great Training Robbery
Hook Your Audience

Pocketfiles

Trainer's Blue Pocketfile of
Ready-to-use Activities

Trainer's Green Pocketfile of
Ready-to-use Activities

Trainer's Red Pocketfile of
Ready-to-use Activities

26.5.05